PROFESSIONAL FICTION WRITING

PROFESSIONAL FICTION WRITING

*A practical guide to
modern techniques*

JEAN Z. OWEN

Boston   *The Writer, Inc.*   *Publishers*

PN 3355
.O 8

Library of Congress Cataloging in Publication Data

Owen, Jean Z.
  Professional fiction writing.

  1. Fiction—Technique. I. Title.
PN3355.O8   808.3   77–188589
ISBN 0–87116–015–3

To
ETHEL E. BANGERT

For thirty-five beautiful reasons

CONTENTS

Foreword   ix

CHAPTER

1   Becoming a Professional Writer   3
2   Establishing Your Writing Habits   9
3   Selecting Your Story Material   15
4   Theme—The Overlooked Factor   24
5   Plot Moves the Story   31
6   Viewpoint Makes a Difference   39
7   Getting Off to a Good Start   48
8   The Important First Sentence   57
9   Creating Lifelike Characters   66
10   The Danger Spot in the Story   78
11   The Art of Painless Flashbacks   83
12   Trouble-Free Transitions   92
13   Tips for Effective Dialogue   99
14   Scene-Planning—Story-Sag Insurance   110
15   Narration and Exposition   116
16   Satisfying Endings   123
17   What Makes a Story Sell?   129

FOREWORD

If a person writes because he must; if nothing can dissuade him; if his life has meaning only when he puts words down on paper, he is already a writer—regardless of whether or not he has been published. Although one learns to write by writing, there are times, especially during the basic learning period, when every newcomer to the profession feels lost and confused. What, he wonders, does one do here? . . . here? . . . and here? It is the purpose of this book to help that writer find some of the answers.

The instruction in the following pages is a distillation of the most meaningful advice I have obtained over the years from editors, critics, teachers, agents, and other writers. Included, too, are examples I have made up to illustrate various aspects of fiction writing techniques. These passages, written as simply and clearly as possible, are not in finished form; if they were to be used in actual pieces of fiction, they would need reworking, revising, polishing.

The process of learning to write never ceases for the real writer—which is what makes the writing profession exciting and challenging. I hope the material in this book will provide the basis for the reader's learning and growing as a fiction writer. It is a wonderful and fulfilling life.

J.Z.O

PROFESSIONAL FICTION WRITING

1

Becoming a Professional Writer

EVERY ASPIRING, unpublished writer longs for the day when he will be a "professional." This is a healthy dream but, in most cases, a beginning writer's idea of the yardstick by which professionalism is measured is somewhat vague. Will he be a professional when he sells his first story? His hundredth? When his income from writing is a thousand dollars a year? Ten thousand? Fifty thousand? When he is able to resign from his present job and devote full time to writing?

Each of these achievements can be a highlight of his career but rarely will you find an established writer who regards any of them as the point at which he stopped being an amateur. Looking back, he realizes that a professional status for a writer is measured by *attitude* rather than by *achievement*.

Putting the reader first

It is important for every writer, especially a beginner, to know and accept this, for it ties in closely with another question frequently asked of experienced writers: "How long does it take a person to start selling his work regularly?" There is, of course, no definite answer to this query; the length of time required is geared to the individual's talent, flexibility, and willingness to work. But this is certain: Whatever his writing goal, he takes an important step toward it

3

the moment he realizes that, to a writer, THE ONLY IMPOR-
TANT PERSON IS THE READER.

Frequently, in preparing articles and lectures for writers,
I use for an example an incident told to me by the friend
to whom this book is dedicated. When her daughter was to be
married, they went to several stores to shop for the wedding
dress. At one place, the bridal consultant was a disinterested
middle-aged woman with wrinkles, sagging jowls, and liver-
spotted hands. As she brought out the merchandise, she ig-
nored her customers; in displaying each gown she held it
under her own chin and preened in front of the mirror, obvi-
ously blind to her own true appearance. She was so enchanted
by the vision of herself as the bride she forgot her true function—and lost a sale she might otherwise have made.

Many writers who smile over this incident are guilty of
the same mistake in their own work. It is, in fact, such a
common flaw that I would be willing to wager that the in-
ability of would-be writers to shift the focus of emphasis
from themselves to their readers has resulted in more literary
failures than all other reasons added together. It permits
the writer to select weak or inappropriate material, to develop careless working habits, and to be deflected from his
mastery of necessary techniques.

Although the professional attitude—automatically and
habitually putting the reader first—can be developed by
some writers more easily and quickly than by others, it is
unlike native talent in that it comes to no one as a "natural
gift." Even the most humble and self-effacing of us must
combat an occasional desire to strut and preen in print, to
push our characters aside as we, ourselves, edge toward cen-
ter stage, where we hope to bask in the admiration of the
reader.

We learn a new word or hear a clever remark, and we are

tempted to incorporate it into the work at hand, even if it doesn't belong there. We have an experience we are eager to tell and, even though we know it is too fragile an incident to sustain a theme, we try to convince ourselves it has such unusual worth that we are justified in attempting to inflate it into a story. We adopt literary affectations in vocabulary, punctuation, and phraseology for precisely the same reason school children stick their thumbs in their ears and waggle their fingers behind the teacher's back—we want to show off in a childish, idiotic attempt to impress our peers.

Too, lack of a professional attitude often results in shallow writing. If, for example, we are portraying a character who is cruel or selfish or jealous, we may find ourselves reaching either for overdrawn stock phrases or for bland, insipid ones, lest we give the reader a peek at our own cruelty, selfishness, or jealousy. Nor is it only our unworthy traits we try to hide; most of us, deterred by an innate emotional modesty, are reluctant to pull back the curtain that hides a display of our feelings when we are gripped by fear, shaken by anxiety, transported by job, exalted by love, or brought to the brink of despair by grief, remorse, or failure.

Not long ago, a student writer, after many months of rejection slips, suddenly began selling almost everything he wrote. When his classmates asked him for his secrets, he grinned and said, "I studied the rules of technique so I could say what I wanted to say skillfully and smoothly. Then I learned to put a lid on the things that are the easiest to write, and I forced myself to explore emotions I would prefer to bypass."

It is evident he has learned that a professional writer must master technique so *the reader* finds the writing clear and easy to assimilate; he has learned not to strut in prose because this bores *the reader;* he has learned to sacrifice the luxury of reticence and force himself to write scenes with emotional impact because this is what *the reader* seeks in fiction.

Developing a professional attitude

Here are a few suggestions that will help the beginning writer speed up the process of acquiring a professional attitude:

1. *Pretend you are Scheherazade when you are working on a story.*

According to the old legend, Scheherazade knew her head would be lopped off the moment the king was bored with her stories. This knowledge gave Scheherazade all the instruction she needed in the art of developing a professional attitude. In a sense, you can avail yourself of the same sort of fearsome help the threat of the executioner gave to Scheherazade. You need not be too concerned about editorial reaction when you are in the throes of getting that first draft down on paper, but when you reach the place where you are cutting, tightening, and editing your story, you may find it helpful to visualize an editor holding your manuscript over the reject bin, ready to drop it in the minute you bore him with incompetent characterization, underdeveloped plotting, and extraneous side excursions.

2. *Don't count on your reader's coming part way.*

Forget that your Aunt Minnie raves about the beautiful descriptions in your letters, that your poetic place cards were the hit of the Christmas party, or that your fellow workers are delighted by your clever editorials in the company news sheet. Even praise by other members of your creative writing group shouldn't be taken too seriously. Admiration stemming from affection and personal association may be heartwarming, encouraging and sincere—but it is almost certain to be hopelessly biased.

The most you can expect from the reader is a willingness to let you prove to him that your story merits his time and interest. He won't make allowances for poor work or finish reading the piece merely to be polite. You must *earn* every scrap of reader identification the hard way, by weighing each word and phrase and by evaluating each scene and plot step in terms of reader appeal.

3. *Accent your qualities of "sameness."*

Although most of us abhor the thought of being peculiar hence our tendency to conform to the current trends of fashion in clothes, hair styles, and house furnishings—there is, in each of us, a strong compelling instinct to emerge from the crowd and be seen as a unique individual.

Do you have traits, viewpoints, and characteristics that make you different from other people? Of course you have, and as you develop your writing skill you will learn when and how to make use of them to the best advantage. But when one is learning the basic techniques of the craft, it is well to remember that no one becomes a professional writer until he has learned to draw upon the universal emotional experiences (and responses) he shares with everyone. These are the fabrics a writer must use to fashion his stories, whether he is writing mysteries, love stories, adventure tales, or science fiction, and regardless of whether they are historical pieces, contemporary tales, or those projected into the future.

Relinquishing a sense of individuality does not come naturally or easily to anyone, but, in a sense, this is a sacrifice every professional writer is called upon to make. When a reader picks up a story or a novel, he wants to read a piece of fiction told in terms of his *own* personal experiences, yearnings, dreams, and philosophies. Most readers are not aware of it (nor would they be inclined to acknowledge it if it were pointed out to them), but the fact remains that they will read a story with interest and enjoyment only as long as their own emotional elasticity can be stretched to encompass it.

Every writer *can* learn to draw upon universal experiences, but many would-be writers are unwilling to do so. I know one woman who has a keen mind, an ability to write sparkling prose, a wide reading background, and a mastery of all the techniques of the craft. But although she has written voluminously for nearly twenty years, she has never been able to sell any of her material. Somehow, she cannot quite bring herself to relinquish her uniqueness, and her constant effort to prove she is "different" is a block that keeps her from communicating. Her work lacks the feeling of involvement, the sense of getting into the character's shoes, which is essential for a reader to feel if the fiction is to be salable.

So, as we approach technique, let's make certain we do not put the cart before the horse by assuming you will become a professional writer by achieving literary prominence. You must become a professional writer by putting the reader first—*then* your stories will sell.

2

Establishing Your Writing Habits

MOST OF today's published fiction has such a smooth, even flow it gives the impression of having been written swiftly, with a minimum of effort. Professional writers know this is an illusion—early in their careers they recognize the truth in the familiar saying: "Easy writing makes hard reading; hard writing makes easy reading."

But even though they accept this fact, most professionals are secretly convinced there *must* be an easier method than their own. For this reason, whenever writers get together, they constantly question each other in search of short cuts and new techniques to ease the creative process.

Amateurs frequently ask experienced writers for advice on working methods: What time of day is best for creative work? Should they write the first drafts of their stories in longhand or should they compose directly on the typewriter? What about a dictating machine? Should they try to write a certain number of words each day or should they work by the hour, paying no attention to the wordage? Is daytime more favorable for writing than night?

There is, of course, no such thing as any one right way to write. It is unlikely that any two people would do their best work in precisely the same manner. It would be foolish for anyone to attempt to force his own temperament, sleep cycle, and working habits to fit someone else's mold, merely

because it works well for the other person. Whenever you
hear of a new working plan or a device that sounds promising, give it a trial run. You will soon learn whether it is
something you should make part of your working pattern
or something you should avoid.

Choosing the right methods for you

But even when you have made your individual choice of the
best working methods, hours, and tools, you should also keep
in mind some general rules which must be part of every working writer's life:

(1) *Read omnivorously.*

Editors, literary agents, teachers of writing courses, work-
shop panelists and lecturers at writers' conferences make a
continuous litany of these two words—READ OMNIVOROUSLY
—yet, too often, the advice is brushed aside by persons who
feel it applies to other writers but not to themselves.

Many aspiring authors rely too heavily on market lists as
a means of keeping themselves informed as to the type of
material "they" are buying. This is a mistake, for although
these market guides, *used correctly,* can be an invaluable
aid in helping a writer find potential markets as well as in
giving him guidelines to use in tailoring his work to conform
to specific demands, they were never intended to be used as
a substitute for reading. In all fields of fiction, there is a
constant, subtle shift in literary style and emphasis; you
cannot keep abreast of these current trends merely by reading a thumbnail list of taboos and requirements.

Although reading is part of every writer's work, it need
not be attacked with grim determination. Relax and enjoy.
Remember that laborious underlining and note-taking are
seldom of value except to make the writer feel virtuous and
scholarly. Occasionally you will need to analyze a story or

novel to study all or part of its construction, but, for the most part, you can sit back and let written words pour into your mental blender. Impressions, nuances, bits of characterizations, pithy similes and pungent descriptions all swirl together, along with your real-life experiences and observations, to make a rich, thick mixture of knowledge from which you draw material for your own fiction. Too thin a mixture results inevitably in writing that is outmoded, weak, or fragmentary.

(2) *Keep regular working hours and try for daily consistency of effort.*

Sporadic writing is all right for dabblers and pretenders; professionals work in a businesslike manner. They reject, once and for all, the idiotic notion that writers work only when they are "inspired."

As with all labor, there are good days and there are bad ones. At times the words seem almost to flow onto the paper of their own accord, and a writer is wise to make the most of such sessions, for they are averaged out by the unproductive periods when it would seem easier to chisel the words out of solid rock. But, for the most part, the moral of the old tortoise-and-hare fable applies to a writer's routine. A slow, steady swing at it, day after day—*that's* how stories and novels are written!

(3) *Don't "talk out" your story.*

Get it down in rough draft, at least, before ventilating it with spoken words. If you must obtain or verify information, tell your informant only as much of the story as is absolutely necessary to give him a clear picture of what it is you want from him.

I once heard a fine novelist point out that there is a certain pre-measured emotional force built into each story idea worthy of writing. If the author expends this force in verbalizing, the task of writing will be far more difficult. Often the story takes on a forced, labored tone.

(4) *Don't feel you must end a chapter or a scene before you stop work each day.*

If you have trouble priming your literary pump at the beginning of each writing session, try to stop work in the middle of a portion that is moving along easily. Then, when you pick it up the following day, you usually find you can get into production more quickly. Many writers, too, find it helps them slide into the rhythm and mood of the story if they start each day's writing session by clean-copying the previous day's output.

(5) *Use your subconscious mind.*

It has been proven scientifically that your brain will continue to hack at a problem while you sleep, so put it to work. Just before you drift off, think about the portion of your story that has you bogged down. When you awaken, you may find you can handle the troublesome spot with no further difficulty.

(6) *Try to accept the fact that occasionally life holds up a stop signal to every writer.*

Births, deaths, weddings, divorces, graduations, job changes, vacation trips, illnesses, moves to new quarters—these are only a few of the crises which come occasionally to everyone. When they occur, there is nothing much you can do but put your writing aside for a time. When an interruption of this type takes place, ride it out with as much patience as you can. *But—*

(7) *Don't look upon every little impediment as a stop sign.*

Many years ago, in one of her novels, Bess Streeter Aldrich wrote a moving account of a woman who came as a bride to a Midwestern homestead. The young wife dreamed of someday putting down on paper all the exciting ideas that pushed at her, begging to be written into stories. But there never seemed to be just the right time to begin work, so, while she waited, she carefully ironed and cut to size all the wrapping paper that came to the house, readying it for use for her rough copy when she would be free to write. And finally the time came—the farm was self-sustaining, the children had been raised and were gone, the house was equipped with modern labor-saving conveniences. Now, at last, she had the leisure. But when she tried to write, the words would not come. Over the years, her talent and creative drive had atrophied from disuse; all she had left of her dream were stacks of brown paper that would remain forever blank.

That novel is of a bygone era; it is improbable that any writer now living ever cut wrapping paper to use for manuscripts—but the story holds out a warning still valid today. The same heartbreaking experience continues to be shared by talented persons who wait too long to begin writing.

If you want to write, get on with it *now*, even though you can't see how you can salvage enough time from your busy schedule to make it worth the trouble. Even a few minutes daily working time can, if well utilized, result in an impressive number of written words in a year.

Some writers can work in odd moments snatched during the day; others, who need a longer span, arise earlier in the morning, or go to bed later at night. However you adjust your schedule, you are certain to discover that working time is easier to find, once your story or novel is well launched, for it begins to make demands that will not be denied, and your routine will, somehow, magically adjust itself. *The important thing is to get started.*

One final reminder: There seldom is, for anyone, a time when it is *easy* to write. If you don't have a sincere desire to do so, you can always dredge up any number of good, logical excuses to keep you from your typewriter. Whether or not you are going to be a writer is not, unfortunately, something you can decide once and be done with it. It's a choice you must make daily—sometimes several times daily—for the entire span of your writing life. It boils down to this: People who dream of becoming writers look either for time to write or excuses *not* to.

Do *you* want to write? Do you—*really?* Then you can!

3

Selecting Your Story Material

ONE DAY back in the Stone Age, a certain man, stirred by a mysterious, persistent impulse, picked up a sharp rock, and on the wall of his cave chiseled some symbols, which, loosely translated, meant: *I hunted a bear. I killed the bear.* In the next cave another man, hearing the hammering, came over to see what was going on, eyed the writing on the wall—and its author—with a mixture of admiration, suspicion, and curiosity, and emitted a series of grunts meaning, "Tell me, where do you get your ideas?"

And so it has gone ever since. For as far back as writers have recorded the vicissitudes of their professional lives, the most common question asked of them is, "Where do you get your ideas?"

Non-writers do not know, as writers do, that *getting* ideas is the easy, *fun* part of their work. It's when one starts *developing* the idea, getting ready to turn it into a story, that the going gets rough.

What is a valid idea for fiction?

The first task confronting the writer is a rigid examination of the idea to make certain it is valid fiction material. The first—and most important—analysis concerns the author's own feelings.

15

(1) *The idea must excite the writer.*

Unless the idea grabs him and refuses to let go, he can relinquish any hope of selling the finished product. The editor of one of the major slick magazines once remarked that the author's enthusiasm forms the girders of the invisible bridge that must exist between story and reader. No matter how technically perfect the story may be, if this one factor is lacking, the piece will fail to sustain the reader's interest.

At some time or another during their careers, most writers attempt to write with borrowed enthusiasm, only to discover that this rarely can be done successfully. Too often, this is what happens:

Writer A, whose "specialty," let us say, is light satirical fiction, has been having a run of rejections, and he casts a wistful eye at the sales record of a friend, Writer B, who has been doing well with spy-and-foreign-intrigue stories.

When Writer A mentions the fact that he is having a bleak time and he thinks it is time for him to try another type of fiction, Writer B agrees. "They're wide open for the kind of story I do," he assures Writer A. "Let me give you a few pointers I've picked up. With all your writing experience, you should be able to sell as many as you can write."

With high hope, Writer A sets out to work on a story idea that is technically perfect but for which he feels no stir of excitement. He writes mechanically, meticulously following the guidelines and skirting the taboos his friend generously points out to him. But, almost always, the story is returned, while Writer B's material continues to sell. Writer B, if exceptionally discerning, may have the uncomfortable feeling that in A's fiction there is *something* lacking he can't quite put his finger on, but usually both writers are blind to the basic difficulty, since the magic ingredient of enthusiasm is fused into the rhythm, pace, and tone of the entire piece and cannot be isolated or pinpointed.

This does not mean that a writer should never experiment or try different material. Quite the contrary. A writer must always be alert to new markets and new trends. But he is wise to work in areas where he feels a strong sense of identity and which produce story ideas that generate enthusiasm within him. Unless he has this at the onset, it is virtually impossible for him to write a story that will draw forth a matching emotion in the reader.

(2) *The idea must be one the author believes.*

As with enthusiasm, sincerity is woven invisibly into the very fiber of the story. The presence or absence of this subtle, pervasive quality often makes the difference between success or failure in marketing the finished story. (Or in making repeat sales to a market, which is infinitely more important!)

Literary honesty is usually harder to achieve than personal integrity. This is because writers possess a keen sensitivity to the moods, thoughts, feelings, and opinions of other people; they are sometimes inclined to undervalue their own opinions and reactions. Consequently, they are tempted to base stories on beliefs of people they admire rather than on their own convictions.

I know how perilously easy it is to fall into this trap, for I have on occasion been caught myself. For example, one ill-begotten story, over which I labored many futile hours, was based on the premise that a woman is miserable and unfulfilled unless she has her man, her cave, and her baby. At the time I wrote the story I was spending several hours each week in a volunteer service organization comprised of a group

of women who repeatedly expressed this opinion. I admired
the women; most of them were older and more brilliant than
I, and I was quite sure they spoke from deep, time-tested
convictions. I also knew that for me, personally, this pattern
of life was necessary for my own happiness. But, down deep,
I did not really believe then, any more than I believe to this
day, that the wifehood/motherhood route offers the only
path of happiness for *all* women.

I submitted the story, over and over, and a number of
editors wrote very nice letters when they returned it. They
complimented me on my writing style and invited me to submit other manuscripts, but they were returning *this* one because it seemed "lacking in motivation" or "did not seem
to focus sufficiently." None of them came right out and said
it lacked the ring of conviction, but I know now that this
was its fatal flaw.

Once, in speaking to a writers' group, I mentioned this
hazard. Later, a timid little woman came up to me and said,
"But how do you know if what you believe is really true?
How can you be certain you are always right?"

You can't. You can be sure only of your own feelings and
beliefs at that particular time—but that's enough. When
Shakespeare wrote, "To thine own self be true," he pointed
the way to establish a foundation of integrity in writing as
in other aspects of living.

(3) *The idea must not attempt to settle a personal
     feud . . .*

For several years, until a critic uncovered my error, I
unconsciously dragged an old childhood grudge into every
story I wrote. The woman who had been unkind to me had
long since moved out of the orbit of my life—out, that is,
except for the fact that I kept trying, through my fiction, to

settle, again and again, a score that time had long since settled for me.

If mine were an unusual or isolated case, I would put it down to a personal idiosyncrasy and not worth mentioning. Unfortunately, however, many writers make this same mistake. They sense, instinctively, that a story needs the propelling force of a strong emotion to make it move forward, but they are not selective enough in choosing the *source* of the emotion.

Even experienced writers sometimes fall into this trap. A well-known and beloved writer of this century wrote with increasing skill and depth, and it is possible she could have become one of the great writers of our time had it not been that a crisis developed in her marriage, and she refused to give her husband a divorce. The resolution of her personal affairs was (or *should* have been) her own business. But from that time on, her stories disintegrated into a thin, repetitious triangle plot in which the wife always managed to defeat the scurrilous "other woman." For several years, because of her tremendous following, the author's stories continued to be published, but eventually her audience lost interest and drifted away and what might have been a legacy of fine, lasting work disintegrated into nothing.

(4) . . . *Or to pay tribute to a person the writer admires.*

Just as you cannot use the reader as a listening post for your grievances, you have no right to ask him to help you pay homage to someone you love and admire, unless you are able to portray the character so realistically he comes alive in print. This takes more skill than most beginning writers possess.

Not long ago a young woman brought me a portion of her

book-length fiction manuscript, rejected by more than a dozen publishing firms.

"Look at these letters from the editors," the author said despairingly. "Every one of them has asked to see anything else I write, but not one is interested in publishing *this* book. If I can't sell *this* story, which is taken from the true-life account of my grandparents, how can I possibly hope to sell anything else?"

I skimmed through the manuscript and saw at once why the editors had invited her to submit other material. Her writing exhibited a fresh, smooth vitality that promised well for her literary future. But, in spite of her ability to express herself effectively, the material at hand was dull and fragmentary, totally lacking in reader identification. The main characters were overdrawn and unreal, possessing superhuman wisdom and angelic virtue, while those who opposed them were melodramatically sinister. Instead of evoking honest, heartwarming sentiment, the pages dripped nauseating sentimentality.

Had this rejected novel been written by another person, I am certain the author would have seen the flaws and weaknesses before she had leafed through more than two or three pages. That she was completely blind to them in her own work, points up a universal truth: Most of us tend to see our own families or personal friends through a haze of bias, affection, and admiration that clouds our perception. And our mental picture of the happiness our work will bring to the subject of the story blurs our vision further. We bask in this anticipated joy instead of maintaining a professional attitude and focusing on the reader.

This does not, of course, apply to everyone whose first literary effort uses a relative or a close personal friend as a protagonist. Some notable stories or books of this type are

Mama's Bank Account, by Kathryn Forbes; *Little Britches,* by Ralph Moody; and *Life with Father,* by Clarence Day. If you feel strongly impelled to produce a story of this type, even though you are new to writing, you should give it a try. The market is always open for a good, warm, family story, for well-written ones are difficult to find. But if, after giving your story your best effort, you find you have difficulty marketing it, you should not feel you will never be able to sell anything because your "best" has been rejected. In reality, your next story is likely to be much better!

(5) *The story idea must be original or at least not imitative.*

A number of years ago, when Jean Kerr's hilarious book, *Please Don't Eat the Daisies,* was at the top of the best-seller list, I happened to walk into an editor's office as the morning mail arrived. I was appalled at the sight of the stacks of manuscripts and commented on the tremendous amount of work it meant for the staff.

"Oh, it's not as big a job as it seems," the editor said cheerfully. "At least half of them, these days, are inexpert imitations of the Kerr book. Apparently people have said to themselves, 'If *she* can write a successful book out of *her* family experiences, I ought to make a mint with mine!' When will writers learn to search for fresh new ideas and write in their own style instead of imitating others?"

When indeed?

(6) *The ideas must contain the major story elements.*

Many story ideas that seem appealing and workable at the outset prove too weak to sustain a story. There are a number of additional factors that must be brought into focus during the writing, but, generally, a writer should feel encouraged to proceed with the material if it contains, *or if it can be molded to contain,* three vital elements:

(a) The plot must incorporate a theme.

(b) The action must result in an *important* change in the life of the main character or characters. Either the situation changes or the protagonist's attitude toward the situation must change. Unless this happens, you don't really have a story—you have a sketch, which is usually extremely difficult to market.

(c) The change must come as the result of deliberate decision and/or action on the part of the protagonist. It cannot be achieved through coincidence, intervention by a kindly Providence, or an accidental stroke of good fortune.

Formula out, structure in

These three elements are sometimes difficult to work into a story, and beginners frequently ask, "Don't these requirements turn it into a 'formula' story? I want to be free to write as I please, to get away from old hackneyed plots, and to develop artistically."

Fair enough. In most of the better markets, the old rigid formula fiction of the thirties and forties *is* gone and is unlikely ever to return. Happily, the trend is away from the predictable, Never-Never-Land fiction; stories now sought are based on more realistic situations and depict more honest emotions than the stories of some years ago. But although rigid story *formula* is out, story *structure* remains. The basic framework of storytelling (which has come down through the ages and is still as valid for the modern writer as it was for Shakespeare, Tolstoy, and Hemingway) does not inhibit anyone from developing his creative ability. On the contrary, it actually helps him utilize his material to the best advantage and frees him to develop his own distinctive style.

Writers working without structural guidelines frequently find that the storyline is not strong enough to hold the reader's interest past the first sentences. Or the story seems to flatten out midway. Or the denouement is anticlimactic. Even *with* the help of structural guidelines, you cannot always be sure if the story will be complete, rewarding for the reader. But this much is certain: if you measure your story material against the six qualities we have outlined and if it seems to meet these requirements, it is viable and promising enough to warrant your working to develop it. Your story is on its way.

4

Theme—The Overlooked Factor

INEVITABLY, AS a writer develops creative skills and occasionally has his fiction accepted for publication, he experiences growing appreciation for writing techniques which help him present his material more effectively. Usually, he listens respectfully whenever anyone discusses characterization or dialogue or viewpoint, and he is likely to genuflect mentally at the mere mention of plotting. But for many aspiring writers, the subject of theme is brushed aside as being inconsequential.

This was my own attitude some years ago when I met the fiction editor of a leading slick magazine. Her magazine had published some of my short stories, and she expressed an interest in the possibility of my doing a magazine-length novel. I jumped at the chance to discuss it with her. I started work at once on a story idea; I put my notes in order, prepared an impressive dossier on all the major characters, and labored over an elaborate outline.

After we had visited a few minutes, the editor said, briskly, "What's the theme of your novel?"

"Theme?" I asked, puzzled, and continued, "I haven't really thought much about a theme. But the storyline is very strong and—"

"Unless it has a theme," the editor interrupted firmly, "unless it all adds up to *say* something—you don't really have

the observation is made through the thoughts or speech of one of the characters, *never* through your exposition. The more subtly theme is presented, the better.

Story idea first

Once a writer is convinced of the importance of the theme, the question arises as to when he should deal with it—before or after he begins to hammer the plot into shape? Here's a danger spot: If the theme comes first, the writer may be improperly motivated, for the chief purpose of any story is to entertain the reader. If you write it primarily to prove a point, it may very well come through as a "preachy" piece of fiction, with the moral spelled out as blatantly as in the old morality plays.

For most writers, the best time to deal with theme is after the original story idea, coming either from a colorful character or an intriguing situation, has impinged upon your consciousness and you have a vague, general idea as to where you want the action to lead the reader. Then, before you begin to manipulate the plot, you are at the ideal place at which to stop and determine exactly what it is you want the story to say. The theme should be neither too wide nor too narrow but should be scaled to fit the dimensions of the story itself. Let's see how this works in a sample plot:

Summary

Donald M., who vowed as a poor boy that he would someday be rich and successful, has permitted his dream to get out of hand. Goaded by his driving ambition, he has become increasingly ruthless and conniving, taking unfair advantage of everyone. Finally, in order to get rid of a fellow employee who stands in the way of his promotion, he resorts to a cold-blooded murder, using a glass paperweight as a weapon. Later, when he is talking to an associate, he lets a remark slip that he fears will reveal his guilt. Afraid of exposure, he picks up the same paperweight to kill the associate. But the paperweight had been cracked when he committed the first murder; now it crumbles in his hand. Momentarily thrown off guard by this occurrence, he is overpowered by the man he is trying to kill. He is brought to justice for his misdeeds.

(Admittedly, this isn't a very good story, but we're merely trying to demonstrate a point of technique, and oversimplification is best suited for this purpose.)

A too-broad theme: *Crime does not pay.*

This is so general a statement it extends far beyond the scope of the plot.

A too-narrow theme: *A person should never choose a glass paperweight for a murder weapon because it might break.*

This bit of information, while true, is not likely to do much toward helping you write a more compelling story.

Now let's try another one: *Ambition, if permitted to distort one's sense of values, can lead to ruin.*

Ah, *now* we have it! Every reader knows people whose drive toward success causes them to be unscrupulous. Also, it is likely that everyone who has ever struggled toward a goal has had at times to hassle with his own conscience to keep from pushing aside those individuals who stood in his way. We have reader experience here for both the villain *and* the victim—a bonus that adds to the emotional impact. The writer working from this theme would know exactly where he was heading, extraneous material could be lopped off, the storyline would remain focused instead of splaying out in different directions. Result: reader satisfaction.

The right emotional tone

Along with giving the writer automatic direction and control of the plot, theme serves still another vital function.

Correctly used, theme can, when needed, change the emotional tone of the story to such an extent it can sometimes salvage a piece of work that might otherwise be lost.

John Fante demonstrates this principle in his famous short story, "Helen, Thy Beauty Is to Me," originally published some years ago in *The Saturday Evening Post,* reprinted in a number of anthologies, and considered by experts an example of superior prose.

The story is of a young, itinerant Mexican fruit-picker who fell in love at sight with a blonde dance hall girl. He was so enamored he gladly spent his bus fare for one more turn around the dance floor with her, even though it meant walking miles back to the labor camp. During this dance, he asked her to marry him, and she, only half hearing him, jokingly agreed. During the following months, as he traveled from place to place, the fruit-picker worked and scrimped, denying himself all but the barest necessities of life in order to save for what he thought was to be his marriage. A year later, when he returned to the dance hall to claim his bride, he discovered she did not remember him.

The skeleton of the story, as summarized here, is downbeat and depressing. In its complete, published form it is not so, even though, from the first paragraph to the last, the reader's heart breaks for the young man. You feel you cannot bear to witness his inevitable disillusionment, yet when it comes, there is an indefinable lilt and upbeat.

Asked how he had achieved this, John Fante answered, *"Theme."* When he started work on the story, he said, his theme was a vague "Reaching for the stars doesn't hurt anyone." But before he had written more than a page or two, he realized it was emerging as a heavy, lead-footed piece. This was not the way he had envisioned it, so before he continued his work on the story, he stopped and, in his own mind, clarified the theme to be: *If you reach for the stars, you cannot help but grow in stature.* At no place in the story will you find these words—not even a veiled allusion to them. But it surges through every paragraph, every sentence, subtly changing the story from a study in futility to an unforgettable experience in sharing the ability of the human spirit to endure. You know that in spite of his bitter disappointment the young man will not be defeated by the experience. The year of "reaching" has increased his stature; he will stand. And you, the reader, will stand with him—a little taller than before.

The shifting of theme in the Fante story points up another important tip: *Don't* feel you must stick with a theme merely because originally it seemed to be the logical one. Sometimes, as you work, you may find a new, stronger premise pushing at you. While you cannot work with *two* themes, feel free to switch from one to the other, if it seems indicated. Just make certain that the part you have already written conforms to the new theme. If it doesn't, go back and start over. You'll save time, in the long run.

Once you become accustomed to working with a theme, you will wonder why you ever looked upon it as a nuisance or a restriction. You will know it for what it is: a valuable, time-saving aid. And you'll be grateful.

Now let's back up a bit. We were talking about the neces-
sity of your giving the characters in your stories a *big*
problem. This is important. Remember: a *big* problem. Every
editor I have ever talked to about this tells me that an in-
credible number of stories are rejected every year because the
problems are too slight. Many of these stories are beautifully
written, with clever dialogue, expert characterization, sparkling prose. But, unfortunately, they are concerned with trivial
items, such as whether or not families will take a vacation, or
if a girl can have a new dress for a party, or if a boy will be
able to borrow his father's car.

Make certain you confront the main character with the
largest possible problem, an almost impossible hurdle to over-
come—one that promises to have a far-reaching effect on the
protagonist's life.

Whenever I give this warning to a writers' group, I can
count on having at least one person challenge my remarks.
How, that individual argues, can I explain the fact, then, that
in the lead story in last month's such-and-such magazine, the
problem was a *very* small one—and a beautiful, heart-tugging
story it was, too!

The answer to this is that when a good story revolves
around something inconsequential, that particular goal, incident, or challenge is not the *real* problem but is merely sym-
bolic. For instance, the three examples of problems about the
vacation, the dress, and the car are, of themselves, too trivial
to be worth writing about. But let's take another look at them
and see how the same situations acquire added depth when
they are reflections of larger problems:

Small: The members of a family want to go on a vacation
because they are bored at home and want a change
of scenery.

Large: A family wants to go on a vacation because one of the members of the family is losing his eyesight and they want him to see beautiful scenes to remember through the years of darkness ahead.

Small: A girl wants a new dress to wear to a dance because she is ashamed to have her friends see her in a dress she wore to the prom last year.

Large: A girl wants a new dress to wear to a dance because her wardrobe has always consisted largely of hand-me-downs from an older sister who has an entirely different type of personality. Our girl longs for her own sense of identity; recognition by her family and friends, of herself as a person.

Small: A boy wonders if he will be able to borrow his father's car because he wants to impress his girl friend.

Large: A boy wonders if he will be able to borrow his father's car; the son has been on probation for possession of drugs. If he gets the car, it will indicate to him that he has earned his father's trust once more.

In the three "large" examples, you can see that the problem is not the vacation or the dress or the car—the actual problem is how to ease a loved one's approaching blindness, how to win a feeling of identity and recognition, how to regain lost trust and reestablish one's self-respect. In any of these three stories, a writer with any imagination could dredge up another gimmick to replace the vacation, dress, or car and still have the same problem, the same story.